THE CULTURE AND CRAFTS OF
MEXICO

Miriam Coleman

PowerKiDS
press

Published in 2016 by **The Rosen Publishing Group, Inc.**
29 East 21st Street, New York, NY 10010

Developed and produced for Rosen by BlueAppleWorks Inc.

Art Director: T. J. Choleva
Managing Editor for BlueAppleWorks: Melissa McClellan
Designer: Joshua Avramson
Photo Research: Jane Reid
Editor: Marcia Abramson
Craft Artisans: Jerrie McClellan (p. 7, 13), Eva Challen (p. 19), Jane Yates (p. 25)

Photo Credits:
Cover top left Irina Afonskaya/Shutterstock;cover top middle left Ariena/Shutterstock; cover top middle right dubassy/
Shutterstock; cover top right ChameleonsEye/Shutterstock; cover middle Joshua Avramson/Shutterstock images; cover
bottom left, p. 21 right morozv/Shutterstock; cover bottom images, p. 6–7, 12–13, 18–19, 24–25 Austen Photography;
cover top, title page top Aleksandar Mijatovic/Shutterstock; back cover, p. 4 top Arid Ocean/Shutterstock; title page cdrin/
Shutterstock; p. 4 bottom Ana Vasileva/Shutterstock; p. 5 left Frontpage/Shutterstock; p. 5 middle Patryk Kosmider/
Shutterstock; p. 5 right jejim/Shutterstock; p. 8 top tipograffias/Shutterstock; p. 8 bottom, 15 left, 15 right, 28 top
AlejandroLinaresGarcia/Creative Commons; p. 9 Stanislaw Tokarski/Shutterstock; p. 9 top Travel Bug/Shutterstock; p. 10
top, 10 bottom, 11 right S Pakhrin/Creative Commons; p. 11 left Lee Snider/Dreamstime; p. 14 left Wolfgang Sauber/Creative
Commons; p. 14 right Creative Commons; p. 16–17 top Ef-av/Creative Commons; p. 16 right Brizardh/Dreamstime; p. 17
right Anna Penigina/Dreamstime; p. 20 top, 21 middle fototehnik/Shutterstock; p. 20 right Kartinkin77/Shutterstock; p. 21
left Raystormxc/Creative Commons; p. 22 top Ahmet Ihsan Ariturk /Dreamstime; p. 22 bottom Jesus Cervantes/Shutterstock;
p. 23 left Uli Danner/Dreamstime; p. 23 right Susanne Neal/Dreamstime; p. 26 top Richard Gunion/Dreamstime; p. 26
bottom left JeniFoto/Shutterstock; p. 26 bottom right Binh Thanh Bui/Shutterstock; p. 27 left MilaCroft/Shutterstock; p. 27
middle Piyathep/Shutterstock; p. 27 right bonchan/Shutterstock; p. 28 bottom Vladimir Korostyshevskiy/Shutterstock; p. 29
left Photo Works/Shutterstock; p. 29 right Carlos Soler Martinezv/Dreamstime.

Cataloging-in-Publication-Data

Coleman, Miriam.
The culture and crafts of Mexico / by Miriam Coleman.
p. cm. — (Cultural crafts)
Includes index.
ISBN 978-1-4994-1126-3 (pbk.)
ISBN 978-1-4994-1136-2 (6 pack)
ISBN 978-1-4994-1165-2 (library binding)
1. Mexico — Juvenile literature. 2. Mexico — Social life and customs — Juvenile literature.
3. Handicraft — Mexico — Juvenile literature. I. Coleman, Miriam. II. Title.
F1208.5 C58 2016
972—d23

Manufactured in the United States of America
CPSIA Compliance Information: Batch #WS15PK: For Further Information contact: Rosen Publishing, New York, New York at 1-800-237-9932

Contents

The Country of Mexico

Mexico

Mexico stands at the crossroads of North and Central America. It borders the U.S. states of California, Arizona, Texas, and New Mexico to its north and has had an important influence on the culture in those regions. Its southern neighbors are Belize and Guatemala.

Before the sixteenth century, Mexico was home to many advanced ancient civilizations, including the Olmec, Zapotec, Toltec, Aztec, and Maya. **Conquistadors** from Spain came to claim the land for the Spanish crown in 1519 and Mexico became a Spanish colony for the next 300 years.

The jaguar represents strength and power in ancient myths of Mexico. Modern Mexico chose the jaguar as its national mammal.

Cultural Mosaic

Mexico today is a vibrant mix of many different influences, where the traditions of the Spanish settlers combine with the **indigenous** cultures that are still very much alive today, along with new immigrant groups from all over the world.

Around 113 million people live in Mexico, making it the second most populous country in Latin America and the most populous Spanish-speaking country in the world. Mexico is a Federal Republic, divided into 31 states plus the Federal District, which contains the capital, Mexico City. The wide-ranging landscapes of Mexico include jungles in the south, deserts in the North, snow-capped mountains, active volcanoes, as well as thousands of miles of coastlines along the Pacific Ocean, the Gulf of Mexico, and the Caribbean Sea.

Mexico City was founded by the Aztecs in 1325. They called it Tenochtitlan.

Some cultural dancers wear Mayan and Aztec costumes to carry on ancient traditions.

Craft to Make • • • • • • • • • • • •

Celebrations in Mexico often include piñatas. They are especially popular at birthday parties and during the Christmas season. Piñatas are usually filled with fruit and candy and sometimes peanuts. People take turns putting on a blindfold and beating at the brightly colored piñata with a stick until it breaks and releases a shower of treats.

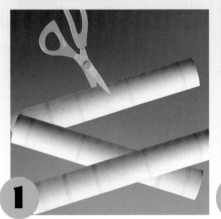

1
Cut three paper towel rolls in half so that you have 6 tubes. (You can also make your own tubes with poster board. Cut the poster board into strips, roll them, and staple them together.)

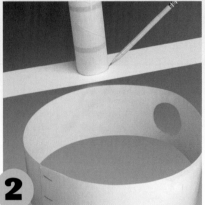

2
Cut a 3-inch (7.5 cm) strip from the long side of a poster board. Lay it flat and place one of the tubes in the center. Trace around it and then cut the circle out. Overlap the ends and staple them together.

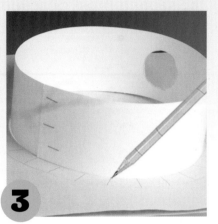

3
Place the poster board band on two pieces of craft paper. Trace around the band with a pencil. Draw another circle about 1 inch (2.5 cm) larger around it. Draw spoke lines between the two circles. Keeping the two sheets together, cut the larger circles out.

You'll Need

3 paper towel rolls
Scissors
Poster board (22 x 28 inches, or 56 x 71 cm)
Pencil
Craft paper (large sheets)
Tissue paper
Fringe scissors, optional
Tape
Glue
Stapler
Small candies
Hole punch
String

4
Using the large circle as a template, cut out two pieces of tissue paper. Make cuts along all the spoke lines of the two paper circles. Fringe the tissue paper.

5
Tape the tubes to the circle spacing them evenly. Make sure one tube is over the hole previously cut out. Place the band over the craft paper circle. Bend the tabs up and tape over them.

·· Piñata

6

Cut smaller circles out of tissue paper in different colors. Fringe the edges and glue all the circles to the front and back of the main circle. Cut a 1½-inch (4 cm) strip of yellow tissue paper from the long side of the paper. Fold and cut a fringe along the bottom. (Use fringe scissors if you have them.) Apply glue to the spokes and glue the unfolded strips.

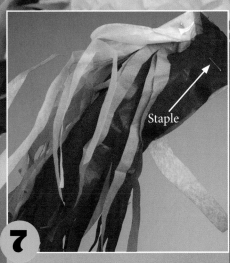

Staple

7

Make streamers by stapling three pieces of tissue paper together. Cut long fringes. Tape the streamers inside the spoke ends. Fill the piñata with candy through the open spoke. Punch a hole in the open spoke. Thread a string through the hole and tie the ends together.

National Holidays

Mexico's colors of red, green, and white can be seen everywhere on holidays.

Mexico celebrates many holidays each year. National holidays include Independence Day, September 16, which celebrates independence from Spain, as well as Constitution Day on February 5, Flag Day on February 24, and Revolution Day on November 20.

Many religious and local holidays also are celebrated. Holiday festivals, called fiestas, are filled with many parades, music and dance, fireworks, traditional foods, and beauty pageants.

Mexico's Independence Day

On the morning of September 16, 1810, a priest named Father Miguel Hidalgo y Costilla rang the church bells in the town of Dolores to call the workers and townspeople to mass. In a speech that came to be known as the "Grito de Dolores," or "Cry of Dolores," he told the crowd that it was time to break free from the **oppressive** rule of the Spanish crown and take back the land that had been stolen from them. Hidalgo's words set off the Mexican War of Independence, which raged for eleven years before independence was finally won.

Mexicans now celebrate Independence Day every year on September 16. On the evening before the holiday, the president of Mexico **reenacts** Hidalgo's "grito" from the balcony of the National Palace in Mexico City. After ringing Hidalgo's bell, the president and the crowd all shout "Viva Mexico!" ("Long live Mexico!"), wave flags, and sing the Mexican national anthem as fireworks light up the sky. Similar celebrations take place in zócalos, or public squares, all across Mexico. On September 16, many cities hold parades and civic ceremonies.

Mariachi Bands

The joyous sounds of Mexican folk music are often heard at festivals, as well as in public squares, at restaurants, and on street corners. The most famous type is mariachi, which started in Guadalajara. Mariachi bands usually include violins, trumpets, several types of guitars, and a Mexican folk harp.

Folklorico dancers wear big hats and colorful outfits for traditional celebrations.

Cinco de Mayo

Many children take part in Cinco de Mayo parades.

Another important national holiday in Mexico is Cinco de Mayo, which means the Fifth of May in Spanish. This date celebrates the victory of a sorely outnumbered Mexican army over the invading French at the Battle of Puebla in 1862. The battle was part of the Franco-Mexican war, which lasted from 1861 to 1867 as France tried to take a piece of Mexico for itself.

Horseback riders portray the cavalry that fought at Puebla.

A Big Day for Puebla

Cinco de Mayo celebrations are at their most festive in the city of Puebla, where the famous battle took place. The city holds a giant parade where thousands of students march alongside soldiers from the Mexican army as well as colorful floats. The city also hosts concerts, folklorico dances, military demonstrations, and reenactments of the Battle of Puebla.

Cinco de Mayo is not celebrated quite as much in the rest of Mexico, and banks and offices are not required to close. It has, however, become a very popular holiday in the United States, where many Mexican Americans mark the day to celebrate their cultural **heritage**.

DID YOU KNOW

The Battle of Puebla is important to world history as well as Mexican history. Nearly twice as many soldiers were fighting for France, but the Mexicans defended their homeland fiercely. Many were not even soldiers, but farmers who used their axes for weapons. The world was shocked when they defeated the mighty French army. Since Mexico's victory at Puebla, no European power has attempted a major invasion of a mainland country in the Americas.

Many U.S. cities with large Mexican communities also celebrate Cinco de Mayo.

Festival performers often shake maracas, a rattle-like musical instrument.

Craft to Make · · · · · · · · · · · · · · · · ·

Maracas are **percussion** instruments often used in the music of Mexico and throughout Latin America. They were originally made from dried gourds with seeds inside that made the distinctive rattling noise.

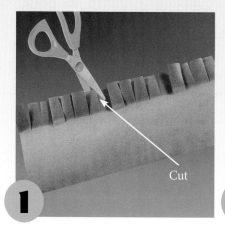

Cut

1

Make the handle of the maraca. Cut out a 7-inch (18 cm) by 12-inch (31 cm) piece of heavy paper. Make a fringe along the top edge by making 1-inch (2.5 cm) cuts about every 1/4 inch (0.6 cm).

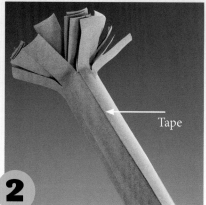

Tape

2

Roll the paper tightly into a tube shape. Tape the tube along the edge.

3

Pour a handful of popcorn kernels through the opening of the papier-mâché ball. Tape over the hole with a small piece of masking tape.

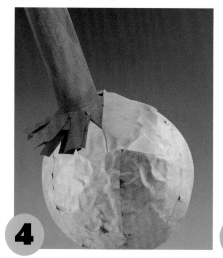

4

Press the handle to the ball so that the fringe spreads out in a circle. Tape the fringe to the globe. Put another layer of tape over the fringe to make sure the handle is secure. Cover the whole ball in tape.

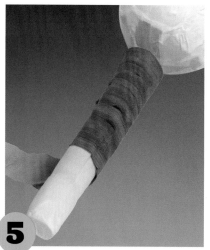

5

Wrap the tube in masking tape. Cut a strip of self-adhesive decorative contact paper or colored tape and wrap the tube from the ball to the bottom of the tube.

You'll Need

Papier-mâché balls (2)
Craft paper
Scissors
Tape
Popcorn kernels
Masking tape
Self-adhesive decorative contact paper or tape
Paint and brush

Maracas

6

Paint the maraca a solid color. When it is dry, add a design such as bright flowers or a cactus. Make a second maraca if you would like to have a pair.

Religious Festivals

All throughout the year in Mexico, cities and villages fill with the dazzling sights, sounds, and scents of religious festivals. Many of these celebrations combine Roman Catholic rituals with traditions that stretch back to **pre-Columbian** times.

Every city, village, and church parish has a **patron saint**, and fiestas are held each year to honor every one of them. Many religious fiestas last for nine days. They include processions, prayers, and candle lightings.

Children may dress as angels or other religious figures.

14

Mexico's Patron Saint

Mexico also has a patron saint for the whole country called the Virgin of Guadalupe. This saint's feast day is December 12, which is called Dia de Nuestra Senora de Guadalupe (Day of Our Lady of Guadalupe). It is one of the country's biggest religious festivals of the year. Hundreds of thousands of pilgrims travel to visit the Virgin's shrine at Tepeyac near Mexico City each year during this time. Many travel on foot from distant villages. Processions, fireworks, prayer services, and song and dance concerts take place in churches dedicated to the Virgin all across the country.

Easter Week, called Semana Santa, is also an important time for religious festivals in Mexico. Many towns hold processions and put on plays with religious themes.

The Christmas Season

In Mexico, the Christmas season begins in November with Advent and ends with a celebration of the Baptism of Christ in January. Beginning on December 16, communities celebrate with Las Posadas ("the Inns"), where children reenact the story of Mary and Joseph's search for a place to stay in Bethlehem.

Children in Mexico traditionally received their presents on January 6 for Three Kings Day, but now many receive gifts on Christmas Day as well.

Every local fiesta has its own traditions, often based on the story of its patron saint.

Christmas trees, a tradition in the United States and Canada, also have become popular in Mexico.

15

Día de los Muertos (Day of the Dead)

Cemeteries are filled with people bringing flowers and other offerings on November 1 and 2.

Every year at the beginning of November, Mexicans honor ancestors and family members who have passed before them on Día de los Muertos, the Day of the Dead.

Día de los Muertos is celebrated all over Latin America, but it is an especially important holiday in Mexico. It marks the belief that the dead can visit friends and relatives on Earth once a year and celebrates the memory of loved ones. Falling over the two Catholic holidays of All Saints' Day on November 1 and All Souls' Day on November 2, Día de los Muertos also has roots in Aztec and other pre-Columbian traditions.

Many people decorate their faces as skulls with paint or masks.

Clay skulls of all sizes are popular holiday decorations.

Music and Memories

Many families celebrate the holiday by cleaning the grave sites of their relatives and decorating the graves with orange marigolds and white orchids while bands entertain the crowds with music. People also honor the dead with special altars called ofrendas that include flowers, candles, food, drinks, photos, and personal **mementos**.

Día de los Muertos is a festive time meant to show that death is not something to fear and is a natural part of life. Images of skeletons and skulls are shown having fun and dancing.

Skull decorations, called calaveras, appear everywhere on Día de los Muertos. You can even find them in the form of brightly-colored candy skulls, and many people paint their faces with skull designs or wear skull masks during parades and parties.

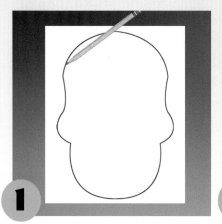

1 On white card stock, draw a skull shape.

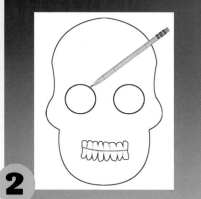

2 Draw a line for the mouth. Draw teeth above and below the line. Draw two large circles or hearts for the eyes.

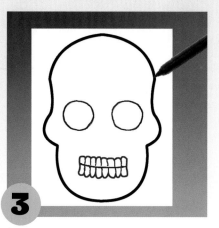

3 Outline all of these shapes and the skull with a black marker. Make the line around the skull thicker than the others.

4 Draw designs on the mask with black marker. Fill in the designs outlines with colored markers. Have fun being creative!

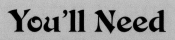

5 Cut around the skull outline with scissors. Use as a decoration or make a mask with it. Cut small holes in the eyes. Cut a hairband in half and tape or staple each end to the back of the mask.

You'll Need

- White card stock
- Pencil
- Fine line colored markers
- Scissors
- Hairband
- Tape or stapler

Traditional Architecture

Historic sites such as the Pyramid of the Moon preserve the Aztec style of building.

Mexico is home to a rich architectural tradition stretching back more than 2,000 years. Ancient civilizations including the Aztecs and the Maya built spectacular pyramids, palaces, and ball courts long before the Spanish arrived. You can see the remains of their great cities at archaeological sites such as Teotihuacan, Chichen Itza, and Uxmal.

When the Spanish came in the sixteenth century, they destroyed much of the indigenous architecture and replaced it with the **Gothic** and **Baroque** styles popular in Spain. They built grand mansions and cathedrals that stand today as some of the most beautiful in the world.

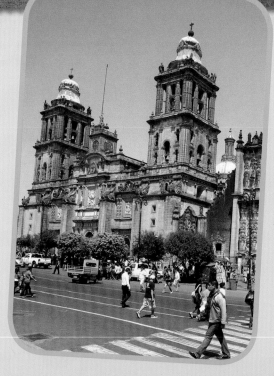

The massive Metropolitan Cathedral in Mexico City was built from 1573 to 1813.

20

The Modern Era

In the late nineteenth century, Mexico's **dictator** Porfirio Diaz oversaw a boom in the construction of public buildings in the French style called Beaux Arts. Many elegant theaters and opera houses were built during this period. After the Mexican Revolution in the early twentieth century, the country's leading architects took inspiration from Mexico's pre-Hispanic roots in a movement known as Toltecism.

Mexico is now home to many stunning works of modern architecture, including Mexico City's Museo Soumaya, an art museum covered with aluminum panels whose shape is meant to reflect a natural form growing out of the earth.

Ultramodern Museo Soumaya opened in 2011 in Mexico City.

Historians think the geometric Sun Stone was used in rituals.

Make Your Own Aztec Sun Stone Craft

The Aztec Sun Stone, a sculpture honoring the sun god Tonatiuh, was discovered in Mexico City in 1790. Currently on display at Mexico's National Museum of Anthropology, this massive artifact was carved in the fifteenth century.

Carved from a single piece of volcanic basalt, the Sun Stone is the most famous of Aztec monuments. It is also known as the Calendar Stone. All of its symbols relate to the sun and highlight the sun's role in Aztec belief and religion.

Make your own sun stone!

You can make your own sun stone with modeling clay or poster board. If you use clay, make a hole near the top of your sun so you can hang it up with a string after it dries. Paint the dried clay in bright colors.

If you use poster board, cut out a large circle. Use markers to make designs, starting with a large sun circle in the center. Tape the circle to a wall to display it.

Traditional Clothing

Many people in Mexico have traditional clothing that they wear especially for festivals.

Mexico is famous for its beautifully made textiles featuring woven designs and delicate embroidery. These textiles are proudly displayed in the traditional clothing that is still sometimes worn in rural and indigenous communities and at festivals.

Mexico's traditional hat, called a sombrero, has become known all over the world.

In rural areas, people may wear traditional clothing every day.

Lots of Layers

For women, traditional clothing includes several layers, starting with the huipil, a loose tunic that may be woven with intricate patterns or decorated with brightly colored embroidery. The huipil might be worn with a long wraparound skirt called an enredo and a woven cape called a quechquemitl. The rebozo is a long shawl that can be draped around the shoulders or head and can also be used for carrying babies or large bundles.

A typical outfit for men consists of a white long-sleeved shirt, sometimes with embroidery or stripes, and loose-fitting pants called calzones. Men also might wear a serape, a wool cape woven with eye-catching designs that can also be used as a saddle blanket or sleeping bag. The designs might show what community or group its wearer belongs to.

Traditional Ponchos

Ponchos were first worn by pre-Columbian people in the Andes Mountains of South America. They are handy for keeping out rain and sun, so ponchos spread all over South America and into Mexico.

It is easy to make a poncho, too. A simple poncho is just a large piece of fabric with a hole cut in the center for the wearer's head to go through. Most ponchos are more elaborate, though, with hoods, fringe, tassels, and fancy designs. Today, kids and adults all over the world use rain ponchos made of vinyl or other waterproof materials.

Mexico's native peoples often wear lots of bright colors.

Vendors with carts sell ponchos, capes, jewelry, and other accessories.

23

Sombreros are wide-brimmed hats designed to protect against the hot Mexican sun. The name comes from the Spanish word "sombra," which means "shade." Simple sombreros worn for working in the countryside are often woven from reeds. Mariachi musicians wear fancier sombreros made from felt and decorated with embroidery.

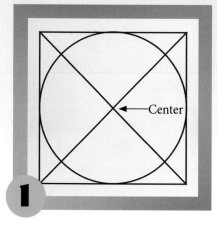

1 Draw a square shape on a piece of poster board with sides measuring 19½ inches (50 cm). Draw diagonal lines from corner to corner to pinpoint the center of the square. Draw and cut out a 20-inch (51 cm) circle from the poster board.

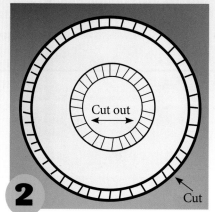

2 Draw a 6-inch (15 cm) circle from the center. Draw a 5-inch (13 cm) circle inside it. Mark lines connecting the circles as shown above. Cut the smaller circle out. Cut along the lines just reaching the edges of the larger circle to form tabs. Lift the tabs up. Fringe the outside of the circle.

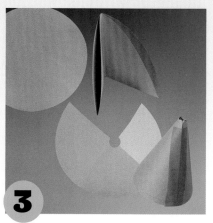

3 Repeat step one on a piece of craft paper. Fold the circle in half, and then in quarters. Cut out one quarter. Cut a small circle from the center. Wrap the circle into a cone shape and tape together. Cover the top of the cone with tape.

You'll Need

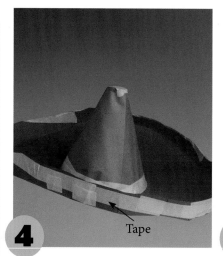

4 Place the cone over the lifted inner tabs of the brim. Tape the cone in place on both the inside and outside of the brim. Press the tabs on the outer edge of the brim up and tape in place.

5 Use paint and paintbrush to decorate your sombrero. Let it dry.

6

Glue pom-pom fringe or pom-poms to the turned-up brim of the sombrero. Tie a ribbon around the hat base.

Mexican Cuisine

Mexico offers many dining choices, from small lunch counters to fancy restaurants.

With a **culinary** tradition that's one of the most popular around the world, Mexicans are passionate about their food. Mexico's markets are packed with a mouth-watering range of fruits, vegetables, and other delicacies, and city streets are lined with stalls selling treats such as tacos, freshly squeezed juices, and seafood cocktails.

Corn has been an important staple of Mexican cuisine for thousands of years. The corn is often dried and ground to make a dough called masa, which is the foundation of many delicious foods. It can be flattened into thin rounds to make tortillas, steamed in corn husks or banana leaves to make tamales, or patted into thicker disks and fried to make sopes.

Corn-flour tortillas can be fried until they are crispy or baked soft.

Hot and Spicy

Beans, squash, avocados, tomatoes, and many tropical fruits were also important parts of the pre-Columbian diet. The Spanish introduced pigs, chickens, cows, rice, and cheese into Mexico, and these ingredients were blended into the country's food traditions. Coastal regions such as the Yucatán and Veracruz make use of fresh fish and shellfish for seafood dishes such as ceviche.

Hundreds of types of chili peppers grow in Mexico, and cooks use them dried or fresh to give food a spicy kick. You can find these chilies in the salsa often served with a meal, or cooked into sauces or stews.

Patriotic Dish

People in Mexico eat chiles en nogada to celebrate their Independence Day. According to legend, the dish was created by nuns in Puebla in 1821 for a fiesta after Mexico gained its independence from Spain. The red, white, and green colors honored the new nation's flag.

To make the dish, a poblano pepper is stuffed with a mixture of shredded pork or other meat, fruit, vegetables, and seasonings. The pepper is topped with red pomegranate seeds, green parsley, and a white sauce called nogada, which is made with cream and walnuts.

Mexican chile dishes are popular all over the world.

Chile peppers come in many shapes, sizes, and degrees of hotness.

Favorite Sports in Mexico

Charreadas, a type of rodeo, are so popular that Mexico declared September 14 as Charro Day to honor the riders.

Horses have long held an important place in Mexican life, especially in the north and west of the country where ranching is common. Mexico's official national sport of charreada, a kind of rodeo, gives skilled horsemen, called charros, a chance to show off their talents. Families gather together at the charreada to watch competitors engage in riding and roping feats, while mariachi bands provide the soundtrack. Every September, the country's best charros and mariachi bands gather in Guadalajara for the Mexican National Charro Championship.

Sporty Nation

Bullfighting, a tradition brought over from Spain, has been popular in Mexico for 400 years. The world's largest bullring, Plaza Mexico, is in Mexico City and seats 50,000 people. The masked fighters of Mexican professional wrestling, which is known as lucha libre, also hold a special place in Mexican culture.

Mexico's true national obsession, however, is soccer. The game was probably brought to the country by British miners in the early 1900s. The Mexican national soccer league has 18 teams, and millions of fans watch the games in stadiums or on TV. The Mexican national soccer team has at times reached the ranks of the world's best.

DID YOU KNOW

Bullfighters are called "toreros" in Spanish. This name comes from the Spanish word for bull, which is "toro." Bullfighting began in Spain in the Middle Ages. The sport spread from there to neighboring France and Portugal, and then to Mexico, Peru, and other places in the Americas. In these countries, the best toreros become famous celebrities.

Toreros wear elaborate costumes. There are toreras, or female bullfighters, too.

Soccer has become Mexico's favorite sport.

GLOSSARY

Baroque A style of European art, architecture, and music from the seventeenth and eighteenth centuries that featured complex decoration.

conquistadors Spanish soldiers who explored and conquered large areas of the Americas between 1500 and 1600.

culinary Having to do with cooking.

dictator One who exercises supreme authority in a country, usually without having been elected to do so.

Gothic A style of making buildings, popular from the twelfth to the early sixteenth century.

heritage The stories and ways of doing things that are handed down from parent to child.

indigenous Having started in and coming naturally from a certain area.

memento Something that serves as a reminder of people or events.

oppressive Cruelly or unjustly using power or authority over another.

patron saint A religious figure associated with a particular place, who is believed to look after the people there.

percussion Musical instruments that make a sound by striking something.

pre-Columbian Relating to the time before Christopher Columbus reached the Americas.

reenact To create something again or to act it out.

FOR MORE INFORMATION

Further Reading

Alcraft, Rob. *A Visit to Mexico.*
Portsmouth, NH: Heinemann Publishing, 2008.

Brownlie Bojang, Ali. *Countries Around the World: Mexico.*
Portsmouth, NH: Heinemann Publishing, 2011.

Landau, Elaine. *Mexico.*
New York, NY: Scholastic, 2009.

Maloy, Jackie. *The Ancient Maya.*
New York, NY: Scholastic, 2010.

Websites

Due to the changing nature of Internet links, PowerKids Press
has developed an online list of websites related to the subject
of this book. This site is updated regularly. Please use this link
to access the list: **www.powerkidslinks.com/cc/mexico**

INDEX